The Blue Boat

The Blue Boat

Selected and Revised Poems

David Lyttle

VANTAGE PRESS
New York

FIRST EDITION

Copyright © 2007 by David Lyttle

Published by Vantage Press, Inc.
419 Park Ave. South, New York, NY 10016

Manufactured in the United States of America
ISBN: 0-533-15440-5

Library of Congress Catalog Card No.: 2006920117

0 9 8 7 6 5 4 3 2 1

To Eulene, my lover, my wife, my home

Contents

Preface

This collection of introspective and philosophical poems is an expression of my personal mythology. One of the main symbols in this mythology is the blue boat. When I was sixteen years old, I built a sailboat in the basement of my parents' home in Chicago. I painted it blue, and my father shipped it for me up to the St. Lawrence River, to our summer home. I sailed my blue boat for many years alone with my alter ego, and raced it against my friends and enemies. Much later, after a hundred poems, the blue boat loomed out of the hazy past as an important symbol in my mythology.

Muriel Rukeyser says somewhere that "the world is made up of stories, not atoms." We live and die by mythology. Christianity is one of the world's great dramatic poems off which our culture feeds, for good and bad. In some of my poems I treat religious symbols and stories as suggestive of eternal dimensions of ourselves. In this semi-religious context I play off against each other the philosophic thought of Jonathan Edwards, the great hell-fire preacher of Puritanism; of Ralph Waldo Emerson, the founder of American Transcendentalism; and of Albert Camus, the European existentialist. I consider these artists and thinkers in chronological order.

Jonathan Edwards, the greatest artist in America before Emerson and Walt Whitman, speaks in his "Personal Narrative" of experiencing "a calm, sweet abstraction of soul from all the concerns of this world; and sometimes a kind of vision, or fixed ideas and imaginations, of being alone in the mountains, or some solitary wilderness, far from all mankind, sweetly conversing with Christ, and wrapt and swallowed up in God." Here and elsewhere he wrote with great beauty and conviction about his experiences of being at One with "God" and nature. I am fascinated by this absolute assurance of the mystic that he has found identity with the very pulse of Being. In my own secular way I have had similar experiences, especially when I was young, sailing my blue boat or sitting in the sun on the worn wooden step of the porch of our old summer home overlooking the St. Lawrence River.

Edwards was also a brilliant artist of a mythology of corporate guilt and hell-fire, a mythology many kind-hearted people do not like to dwell upon. But the recognition of the darkness of experience is necessary for the growth of significant Beauty. I must say, however, that although I respect Edwards for his superb artistry of the negative, I dismiss his doctrines of a vengeful deity, innate sin, and the exclusivities they entail. For example, natural evils (evils not caused by the moral will of man), such as earthquakes, hurricanes, diseases, are not caused by man's "sin," as Edwards says they are. No man can be that evil, only a god who takes his frustration out on the creatures he has created, only a god who, in the name of "Justice," warps the poor and malformed, who lets the innocent drown and twists their bodies into wreckage, who lets the starving and forlorn wander the world.

In Edwards' theology, God is the center, the origin, the sustainer, the predeterminer of every blowing blade of grass in the universe, on whom the individual is totally dependent and whose freedom, if it can be said to exist, resides only in so far as he is an agent of God's will. For Edwards

God also is everywhere present with His all seeing eye. He is in heaven and in hell, and in and through every part of His creation. He is where every devil is, and where every damned soul is: He is present by His power and by His essence. He not only knows as well as those in heaven who see at a distance, but he knows as perfectly as those who feel the misery. He seeth into the inmost recesses of the hearts of those miserable spirits, for He upholds them in being.

Edwards obsessively sought aesthetic symmetry of heaven and hell in his mythology of exquisite Being. In truth, he subliminally became God as he experienced the keen compound of joy and pain as he judged the whole world.

*   *   *

For Edwards, God is All, man nothing; for Emerson it was exactly the opposite: Man is everything, the center and origin of the universe, the reservoir of infinity, and "God," a mere idea. Like Edwards, Emerson was a mystic, a poet, and a philosopher who believed that mind makes matter, not matter, mind. But unlike Edwards, Emerson rejected the idea that there is an infinite God who created the material world. His philosophic question, therefore, was: If mind makes matter and God does not exist, who made the world? He concluded, in speaking about the exploration of the universe by science, that "the aim in all science [is], in the unprofitable abysses of entomology, in the gigantic masses of geology, & spaces of astronomy—simply to transport our consciousness of cause & effect into those remote & by us uninhabitable members, & see that they all proceed from 'causes now in operation,' from one mind, & that Ours" (*JMN* 7:111; 1838). Thus he concluded that *Our* "one mind" made the universe—not just our finite minds but what he called among other things throughout his work the "universal mind," "God," the "Over-Soul," the "soul," "the infinitude of the private man" (*JMN* 7:342; 1840). He wrote: "it is strange that any body who ever met another person's eyes should doubt that all men have one soul" (*JMN* 5:364), an observation which implies his intuitive basis for the principles of sympathy and love.

Further, Emerson's journals also suggest that he conceived this "one mind . . . [of] Ours" to be our Universal *Unconscious*. For instance, he wrote: "God is the substratum of the mind" (*JMN* 12:243) and that "the reason why only the work of genius fits the wants of all ages is because that which is spontaneous is not local or individual but flows from that internal soul which is also the soul of every man" (*JMN* 12:389). His position was that the ground of Being and he were *not* two conscious exclusive entities, but that God is the unconscious ("hidden") dynamic of every finite conscious individual; and furthermore that the content of the unconscious dynamic is projected through the consciousness of each individual and manifested as "the divine dream" of nature. In this way he escaped a philosophy of materialism and, by making the collective unconscious the origin of "objective" nature which we all share, escaped solipsism. Also, by establishing the individual as the consciousness of God and partaker in the creation of the phenomenal world, he was justified in celebrating the individual as deity or, as he wrote in *Nature*, "part or parcel of God." And more: since he held that nature is the expression or language of the unconscious universal, he assumed that man the individual may learn about his "hidden" infinite unconscious by reading nature as symbol (see "The Over-Soul"). This is why he and Thoreau sauntered through the woods and fields: they were reading the harmony of the inner and outer worlds.

Jonathan Edwards called man "a worm," and a hundred years later Emerson recorded in his journal: "In certain moments I have known that I existed directly from God, and am, as it were, his organ. And in my ultimate consciousness Am He" (*JMN* 5:336–37). When he said this he was neither mouthing egocentricity, nor voicing the Quaker belief that God is the still, small voice of conscience in man, nor giving us merely an hyperbole of what he thought are the potentialities of the naturalistic mind. Rather, he was claiming that the ground of Being does not lie outside of ourselves; he was identifying the individual as the very consciousness and dynamic heart of the universe. To support this claim, he often referred to the power of creative inspiration which at times overwhelmed him: "the joy which will not let me sit in my chair, which brings me bolt upright to my feet, & sends me striding around my room, like a tiger in his cage, and I cannot have composure & concentration enough even to set down in English words the thought which thrills me—is not that joy a certificate of the elevation? & consoles all suffering?" (*JMN* 14:308; 1859).

As a prose-poet, Emerson obviously used metaphor to suggest the heart of his religious philosophy, which cannot be conceptualized. In talking about the creation of the world, he described the soul or the universal mind as a spiritual seed from which blossoms our entire universe as idea. "All nature," he noted in his journal, "is only the foliage, the flowering, & the fruit of the Soul and . . . every part therefore exists as an emblem & sign, of some fact in the soul"; and again: "The world flows ever from the soul" (*JMN* 5:366; 7:499). And again, building upon his hypotheses of philosophic idealism and the identity of God and man, he exclaimed in 1840: "I am the Universe. The Universe is the externisation [sic.] of God. Wherever he is, that bursts into appearance around him. The sun, the stars, physics & chemistry we sensually treat as if they were selfexistences [sic] and do not yet see that these are the retinue of that Being we are (*JMN* 7:542). Emerson obviously denies the diminution of man by Calvinism and modern science.

Finally, he stated in his essay "Self-Reliance," a passage which may be incomprehensible to the skeptic but which to me is a cathedral of intuitions:

And now at last the highest truth . . . remains unsaid; probably cannot be said; for all that we say is the far-off remembering of the intuition. That thought by what I can now nearest approach to say it, is this. When good is near you, when you have life in yourself, it is not by any known or accustomed way; you shall not discern the footprints of any other; you shall not see the face of man; you shall not hear any name; the way, the thought, the good, shall be wholly strange and new. It shall exclude example and experience. You take the way from man, not to man. All persons that ever existed are its forgotten ministers. Fear and hope are alike beneath it. There is somewhat low even in hope. In the hours of vision there is nothing that can be called gratitude, nor properly joy. The soul raised over passion beholds identity and eternal causation, perceives the self-existence of Truth and Right, and calms itself with knowing that all things go well. Vast spaces of nature, the Atlantic Ocean, the South Seas; long intervals of time, years, centuries, are of no account. This which I think and feel underlay every former state of life and circumstances, as it does underlie my present, and what is called life and what is called death.

*   *   *

The third philosophic perspective which I find constantly before me is that of existentialism. For example, when I am sailing my blue boat, I sometimes appear to be sailing in the world Albert Camus refers to in *The Myth of Sisyphus*:

> At the heart of all beauty lies something inhuman, and these hills, the softness of the sky, the outline of these trees at this very minute lose the illusory meaning with which we had clothed them, henceforth more remote than a lost paradise. The primitive hostility of the world rises up to face us across millennia. For a second we cease to understand it because for centuries we have understood in it solely the images and designs that we had attributed to it beforehand, because henceforth we lack the power to make use of that artifice. The world evades us because it becomes itself again. That stage scenery masked by habit becomes again what it is. It withdraws at a distance from us. Just as there are days when under the familiar face of a woman, we see as a stranger her we had loved months or years ago, perhaps we shall come even to desire what suddenly leaves us so alone. But the time has not yet come . . . That denseness and that strangeness of the world is the absurd.

This world is more terrible than the Puritan world; it is meaningless, and man is an animal whose essence is meaning. My face pales as I bound in my blue boat over the waves that might as well be made of cement for any personal relationship they have with me. Indeed, the whole inanimate world around me stands denuded and alien before my human consciousness; I intuit no origin and no final home for man or beast. But after a while I am bored and re-dress these white capped waves, this granite shore, this wind and blue sky and flying clouds in the velvet dream of Our universal mind. But then again I am slowly raped of mythology by

Camus, and drift in circles with what Emerson called "the double consciousness" of the real and true.

*   *   *

The shadows in my own art result from my sustained dismay at the pitiful moral condition of mankind. But deeper still I am dismayed at the apparent nature of nature itself; at the meaninglessness of the cosmos; at the pointlessness of time; at the homelessness of infinite space; at the relentless brush of lives into the grave; and so on and so on. Fred Hoyle the great physicist defined religion as "a desperate attempt to find an escape from the truly dreadful situation in which we find ourselves." Stephen Crane cried out about "the unknown appeals of brutes, the screams of cut trees, the senseless babble of hens and wise men—a cluttered incoherency that says at the stars: 'O, God, save us.' " But there is really no one out there to save us—and the material world is *not* all there is; our spiritual home is not among objects, living or dead. Again I drift back to Emerson's assumption that we lie in the "lap of immense intelligence"—which is Our own eternal subjectivity symbolized by the night sky before our own bright eyes.

Today I walk in my garden, and sail upon my waves. I am the consciousness of God of everything that is. I fill the infinite dimensions of my being with stories of unending time and space. And I know that this evening in a dark corner of my garden, Jonathan Edwards will be there, pacing, flickering, tinged with insanity, and that behind him riveted upright in the moonlight will stand the material world in all its colorless absurdity. The fact is, we do not even know whether what we know is all there is to know or only a small part of everything that is. We cannot get out of ourselves to find out. But these lives of ours are great adventures. They are mythologies, mysteries impossible to define. The intelligence of man is the loneliness of man. Atoms are true, but stories are real.

References

Albert Camus: *The Myth of Sisyphus*. Trans. by Justin O'Brien (Vintage: New York 1960), p. 11.

Emerson: (*JMN*) *The Journals and Miscellaneous Notebooks of Ralph Waldo Emerson*, ed. William H. Gilman et al. 16 vols. (Cambridge: Harvard University Press, 1960–1982).

David Lyttle:

"The Sixth Sense of Jonathan Edwards," ~~Hibbert Journal~~ (~~1965~~). The Church Quarterly Review 1966

"Jonathan Edwards on Personal Identity," *Early American Literature* (Fall, 1972).

"Emerson's Transcendental Individualism," *The Concord Saunterer* (Fall, 1995).

"The World is a Divine Dream: Emerson's Subjective Idealism," *The Concord Saunterer* (1997).

"Emerson and Natural Evil," *The Concord Saunterer* (2001).

"Emerson on the Soul," *The Concord Saunterer* (2003).

The Blue Boat

I am not on my Father's
business anymore
but my own.
I never did not exist.
And when I sail high seas
to Hog Island, Red Horse Light
the gray chop talks to me
of those who are not here.
And when I get back
those who prowled around the hut
where I keep my blue boat
muddying doors
smashing padlocks
I will stone
and tear with my nails.

Down Near the Back Road: Secular Epiphany No. 1

I drive to the junkyard
at twilight, and I halt
and look out for myself
hard in the rusty gloom

the dead dead violence
of iron, mangled shadows
and ruin and uselessness
setting my teeth on edge.

I think about my time
my mother and my father
what time has done to me
and will do—death is sure

and the headlights drain
like urine in the grass.
I hunch, and press down.
The outside gathers hurry.

And this loose skull full
of old cars and twilights
what matter does it make?
Where do I go from here?

What is the caring for?
There are so many ways
to care, can hate it all
each minute, and yet care.

I think about this here
uniqueness that I am
this me, this dear spot
this focus of light-years

and cut the cold engine
and get out. And I walk
around to the deep swamp
where what is left slips

into dark water touched
by the night wind, watch
over the water, the small
explosions of moonlight

and hear the chug chug
of the June bullfrogs
like old machinery
half sunken in the mud.

And I am just by myself
at just this moment, here
in the high lucid weeds
down near the back road.

Firewood

I am a collector
of shadows.

I poke
through trash cans
along moonlit roads
on the outskirts
of town.

I camp out
in fragments of wood
near water.

I belong to no school
old or young.

I am an antagonist.
I parry the outside.

But also
            I listen
to the question
standing
in the skies
        with ancient
unretractable brightness
the question
that must be attended to
in the open.

In the woods
I watch myself
    like a dumb cop
        tripping
    falling foreseen
powerless and
flat
      so that
    who am I now
   half risen
in moonlit
water
      my skin
   shining like
tinfoil
      my soft
   nails bending
over stone?

I wait.
I am warm.

My garbage burns
with a black flame.

Something Very Old

"He tasks me; he heaps me; I see in him outrageous strength."

—Ahab

I saw something very old
last week when I was driving
in the neighborhood of north.
It was on the right hand side
of the road, past Watertown.
They say it bulged up long ago
but I had not seen it before—
perhaps it was under the snow.
This is April; it was a lank
gray, irregular outcropping
of Paleozoic granite
in the light green grass
of a meadow, like the scarred
flank of a whale. I would
like to know where it was
before I knew it was there.
It seems to be the center now
of something I cannot forget
and possibly always knew
out of the inflamed corner
of my eye. It is certainly
a testimony against pantheism.
I wish I could drag it out
and shove it off into space
like a great lumpy dirigible.
But that would upset the wild
equilibrium of earth
because it goes down so far

and I don't know if I want to
change where I live right now
that much, or scare even more
what lives out there, beyond
Christmas. But just to think
of it makes me feel out of place.
It makes me remember a few
of my young colleagues at school
and even poor Bartleby who said
"I want nothing to say to you."
It is what makes other drivers
prefer not to move over
in head-on chicken collisions.
It will bug me to the day I die.
I want to drive back some night
to watch its glacial cussedness
and dark scars, by moonlight
stamp on it, and shriek! and
if it moves, dress myself up
in the colored rags of darkness
hop, shake, make sorry noise
and try to voodoo it away.

Confirmation (of the Atomic Age)

I see the moon
and snow like wax
upon the fields
and wonder how we do
and what our chances are
against the slow bomb
of yesterday
and horror
         glares
    like flowers
on each tree.

We cannot be sustained
by that beyond us
not a person in the world
can save us
not any one divine
nailed
       to the past
or screaming
in the dubious future.

We will go
some summer
     in the white
excruciating heat
and I will take you
in the gutted fields
     and show you how
the giant briars
thrive
like fireworks

       how the sun
reeks tadpoles
like rubber
       how it draws
up grass
like iron fillings
       how always over field
and river, in the clear
pathetic distance
stand
       the dark clouds
the flash of storm
       and silence
of the clashing trees.

I will confirm for you
that nowhere where we go on
striding the swarming
surfaces of light
or at night
beneath the sparse
skylight of consciousness
in our beds lying
can we escape.

Mouse

(About opening up in Spring our 100-year-old family summer home on the St. Lawrence River.)

I snowshoed back in late March
over the hills, against the blue war-
cry of the wind thru the tall pines
to the old cottage by the river
vacant, gaunt, without my family
or any consciousness at all?
Inhuman footsteps in the snow
broken limbs, and fangs of ice
crinkled over eaves. I heaved
off the shutter from the front door
and walked right in upon the dark.
The whole cottage was immense
and shady like a lost universe
creaking in the wind. Jumbled
furniture stood on the floor
like a city. I heard my mother's
mother cry upstairs in her room
facing southwest and the river.
The cottage was a cold dark place
left over from the past, a huge
emptiness of mere wood, vandalized
the stairs and kitchen strewn
with the white hair of children.
What was I doing there? Looking
for someone who forgot to leave?
Wailing a curious death of gods?
Seeking something I could feel
worth paying for? I watched
the green mold on a sneaker

two rusty skillets in the sink
crystals growing on a cobweb
a wizened and bedraggled carcass
starved or dead by poison seed.
But then I sensed within the dark
the secret clarity of presence
smell of mouse, the intimacy
of tiny lives bundled
together against the cold.
It was the overwhelming real
here, now, like incense burning.
And the spring light beamed
through the knotholes, lay
golden in the clapboards.

My Father at Ninety-five (1979)

Out of the night
of mist and driving rain
I stand before the traffic
        then step in reflection
into my father's house

and the fine design of my shadow
falls across the parlor floor.

My father, in his blue velvet chair
lies bundled like a cherub.

The energy of a man
is slipping
away without his knowing
down the white electric cord
of the lamp in which light remains
this desiccated mass of intense fragility
this chrysalis, this crowned shadow
this translucent skin, rich veins
old power lines along the arms.

I watched him with my facetted eyes.

He lies there, sentimental, proud
vulnerable, a black patch over one eye
the other clouded less by cataract
than his own landscapes of history—
Kings and Queens, cathedrals in green
English mist, Shakespeare, Voltaire
the Age of Reason and of Light
the new world of Franklin, Paine
and ministers of the free west.

Once a talker of great worth
he had an earnest desire for Peace
for the cheerful brotherhood of Man
for the whitening of Negroes.
A true humanitarian scholar
he had hundreds of friends.

Later, back in my own home
the rain and lightning threaten
all to be lost
and the lamps flicker
with the failure of distant power.
And I wonder, my dear father
with the pain
that may make all things possible
where in your landscape
is that Latin Doctor for the bungled eye
who probes under the dark patch
and where the Pilgrims
who were stuffed like spiders
into their frail ships
and drawn
across the cloudy ocean
by that "Light Unchangeable"
to "a land of wild & savage heiw
with no freinds to wellcome them"?

Note: The quotation at the end of "My Father at Ninety-Five (1979)" is
from Chapter Nine in William Bradford's *Of Plymouth Plantation*.
Its spelling is from the edition edited by Harvey Wish (New York
Capricorn Books, 1962). The phrase, "Light Unchangeable" comes
from St. Augustine's *Confessions*.

The Old Pump

The rain is falling
on the green boathouse
and on the marsh outside
and I am in the green
boathouse, working alone
on the old black water pump
that like a hard muscle
has pumped up marsh water
to the main house longer
than the gibberish
of private myth reveals.
It needs new leathers
like I need a new heart.
What is my life coming to?
I have grunted and sworn
over these iron gears
for forty odd years.
But now it works again
thumping up marsh water
like blood thru lead pipes
to cook food in, to wash
dishes, faces, hands
to flush the toilet.
And now the rain passes
like some useless pain
clarifying nothing
and in the light
of evening
        white moths drift
under the long pink anatomy
of clouds
            and I stand

by a golden boathouse
among lilies and duck-weed
singing to the totems
of my simple life
along the shore
                glancing
thru leaves and shadows
at the main house.

Going Home to Hyde Park for Christmas

I sped west
      for my sake
    and for the sake
of others also
outside
        racing
  the sunset
over the black top
out of the clear void
of darkness
sucking
my insides out—
speeding
        over the flat
    white white plains
of Ohio
        over Gary
  on the skyline
past Whiting
and the steel mills
like griffin
feeding on the ass
of cold Lake Michigan
the blue licking gas
and huge refining
fart of oil—
    speeding north
over the Outer Drive
under the stars, by the long beaches
grey and luminous with heaving ice
and foam
    speeding—

16

toward the loop of Chicago
the tiny skyscrapers
floating like tinsel
in the wind—

swerving
west, and racing
past the utilitarian church
of Science and Industry—

speeding into Hyde Park
to my dear parents
to my first home
still a glowing
center of
perhaps
the only kind
of warm universe
there is
people
of true class
facing
inward in
an open circle
of rare friends.

At night
the old historian
still savagely dutiful
in adoration
in his brown
bathrobe
dragging

the loose smell
of sleep
around his cluttered
yellow sheeted
study
        pausing
    always listening
down the stethoscopic hall
for the slow breathing
of the other one
my mother
    in the back room—
a soft painting
                of blue sky
        white clouds
and flowers.

    There is violence
of loneliness
like space
inside ourselves
that we must fall
back from
into each other's arms.

    I sped west
racing the sunset
        over the black top
tracing the thin white line of sanity—
        going home to say
Good-bye
            good-bye

Rosemary (1975)

> "All things within this fading world hath end."
> —Anne Bradstreet

I used a claw hammer and crowbar
to wreck the green cottage
called "Rosemary"
built by my great Uncle Ed
for my parents
when they were very much in love
and I was six years old.

I clambered to the ridge pole
tore off the roofing like a scalp
ripped up the boards
nails screeching
like teeth hanging to a bone

dug hard putty out of eaves
pulled out torn stockings, rags,
wadded clippings of old news
pink fiberglass packed into holes
against bugs and night wind.

I noticed on a rafter
pitted by a nail—
"July 24 R.A.S. 1930"—
that was my first cousin, sixteen
who pumped, rowed, did chores
called me "Sweetie Pie"
and chased me through the bright fields
when I was bad
and no one else could run as fast as I.

(If ever this house
needed to be torn down
it should have been torn down
years ago)

I swung on the rafters
like an old ape
and peered down
into the two bedrooms
reeking
with secret human experience.

I leaped down, kicked
out the thin inner wall
that had kept many together
and many apart—

            danced back
pried up the floor
straddled the stringers
and looked down
at the first floor, the rubble
of kitchen and parlor—dust
dust of communal living
words, words, words.

(What is the past worth
when I can tear down quick
a house like this?)

Exposed
Under the blue sky!
I sprang to the ground

struck down
with my claw hammer and my crowbar
                the stone chimney
the clapboard walls—
the whole frame shivering.

Gasping, I ripped up
the main floor
found nothing but cobwebs
cedar beams, red puddles
plain dirt
and a low dark place
where a small and missing person
could have lain alone for many years.

What is remembrance for, and constancy?

The cottage was built on a swamp
and it had certainly fallen off
its foundations
long before I began
tearing it down from above.

But it was just a summer cottage
built for my parents when they were young
in the most beautiful country
they had ever known.

I sometimes feel
with parents dead and cousins dying
that I'm the only man left alive.

Nothing on earth is worth keeping forever.

But I see now, now
the rubbish is cleared away
that the space where the cottage stood
is new space to build new worlds in.

But I could have done better things
any day, than wreck this cottage.

                    *   *   *

One winter day I snowshoed back
a crystal ghost, over the white hills
and meadows, down to the shore
where the cottage still stands
gigantic, blocking my view
the reflection
of its equivocal greenness
staining the snow, like grass.

Thanksgiving in the 1000 Islands
of the St. Lawrence River

"As to what is said of the *absolute* existence of unthinking
things, without any relation to their being perceived, that is
to me perfectly unintelligible. Their *esse* is *percipi*; nor is it
possible they should have any existence out of the minds of
thinking things which perceive them."

—George Berkeley (1685–1753)

I could have napped
but I don't go in for naps.
Instead, I toured the Islands
in my motorized blue canoe.
I used an old Johnson 1 1/2
barely horse enough to charge
against the gusty north wind
and flurries of dry snow.

The motor made an awful racket
but I was Leather Stocking hunting
the wooded shore for painted savages
and then La Salle, the first white man
to sail on tip-toe up this mighty river.

I know these islands like a book—
they are my summer home of great
anticipation: kids yelling, dogs barking
colored sails and white caps sparkling
girls tanning and oiling on the dock
and the warm water we enter into
the stormy nights of reciprocity
the lighthouse of our destinies
and then the change of season:

goldenrod, chicory, red leaves
the misty east wind and shivering
the flight of souls abandoning
their summer homes.

I made this journey in my blue canoe
to find out what these islands really are
when summer and all my friends are gone.
I wanted an existential feel of the place
flat out before me, in black and white
like a dictionary drained of meaning.

I churned from one dark finger of land
to another dark finger of land.

The cold water shone like mercury
and splashed on boulders hunched
along the shore. The spotlight
of the waning sun ranged
above the heavy wall of clouds
striking the islands to reveal
the whited trees thrashing
in crowded silence
along the shore
like outcasts of humanity.

I cut the engine, drifted, cried out
but what came back was what
I cried out, cried.

I found that when I am alone
these misty islands are so blank
and drained of meaning, I am tempted
now to push imagination on, like paint

coloring the earth and evening sky
with old religious figures
of repose; but I don't.

Beyond all this, I found
that what these islands are
these forms floating on the water
under the vast night sky, what they are
when kids and dogs and girls are gone
and when my blue canoe and I are lost
forever in a tangled moonlit swamp
I say, that what these islands are
beyond all memory, all dreams
all mythology and metaphor
beyond all consciousness
may be nothing at all.

The Church on Egg Hill

"Sinners in the Hands of an Angry God."
(July 8th 1741)

—Jonathan Edwards

I hustled
on a hard road
in January
rutted
with shadows
up wooded Egg Hill.

The hoarfrosted
meeting house
had a new
galvanized gutter
a leaning
steeple
of warped boards
and pecker
holes
blue sky
showed thru—

an iron fence
circled the graves.

I hunkered down
by a gray batten wall
out of north wind
and heard crows
caw caw
      in bright fields
of evangelical light

and I rose
around a corner
climbed
the long stairs
and picked a latch
into an old religion
gritty with acorns
and dead wasps.

In wavy light
of leaded windows
leaves of sadness
floated
on the sills
and pale lathing
poked out dark holes
a bell-rope
from the ceiling
dangled like a worm
on an icy stove
and twisted pipes
oozed soot
across the pews.

The pews were laid
out like a diagram.

I leaned
forward in the pulpit
and heard
a whispered cry:

"Dear children who
are in an evil world
let me therefore earnestly
exhort you to keep pressing
into that golden kingdom
with all the courage
you are masters of—
Be very diligent
the wrathe abides.
We have no reason
other than to think
that some of you—
you that are out there—
you will be changed soon.
We can conceive
but little
of the matter.
He will have you"

and the white walls
glistened
        with awful wails.

I slammed the door
against vandals

and the sun
was like an angry spider
sinking behind the shadowy hills—
and the scarlet clouds
were flaring
along
the paths of heaven

28

and inside
the iron fence
behind the headstones
casting
white shadows
across the black snow
came Christ creeping
with his tomahawk.

Cotton Mather's Easter

In slanted
gray springlight
the last Mather wanders
along the river bank
near the church
on soil
softening
like thawing meat
sprinkled
with flowers green
and white.

He clenches
his gaunt hands
and his long coat flaps
behind—
        and dreams
of young wandered flesh
stroked firm on racking vines
in the black bewitching heat
of summer nights—

and knows himself lost
seen thru, doomed
to haunt
that last hour
when those few
        chosen after all
will grind out of the loosened ground

and tramp those crisp
and rosy waves
to that sweet shore
where marching saints
loom in the haze
like mica.

He drops
his white skull
into his white hands

and cold outbursts of sun
on gray waters move
like a headache.

The Storm

(*apropos* Jonathan Edwards)

"There are in the souls of men those hellish principles reigning."

We were sitting around the lamp
rocking, in our den, not reading
just looking at the print of books
our eyes averted from each other
and feeling more within ourselves
all the principles of our nature.
Bleak wind outside, and the rain
forgetting the lake's other shore
the waves pealing up over rocks
in frail layers of the gray thing
quick scraping of dead branches
fragments of leaf, like green skin
stuck to the window, Paul's yell
across those awfully broken waters
sweet yellow of scripture scattered
the lighthouse decayed by the rain.
"This world is not our abiding place"
and we were not around the light
but outside, but not together
but outside, in the flaring rain
staring at our faces drawn by age
like wolves, rocking in our chairs
with the dirty redness of our eyes
the wildness of our changing hair.

Tenth of Feb. 1675

"Their glittering weapons so daunted my spirit. . . ."
—Mary Rowlandson

I am pacing
with him
    once more
in Mary's graveyard
on the icy hill
on a cold
clear night.

The city shines
in the valley
like tepees.

I whistle
and brown leaves
fly up
like eyelids

and mounds
of luminous snow
creep
in the wind
like flesh trying
to come back.

I lean on arms thin as grass

and stars glint
in black oak trees
swaying
like chicken bones
or hard veins.

                    Out
of the darkening ranges
flaps a copter
red light on the thorax
snapping
                    like a heart.

My face is painted
with vengeance.

and I am on the warpath
with an arrow and a feather
and a long knife

and I am pressing
in heavy boots after
my dog Peter
in circles
at night
on the icy hill
around the gravestone
of my own Mary
scalped
        long ago
in bright moonlight
by all the pale Indians
of the world.

The Problem of Here

"I said when I awoke, 'After some more sleepings and wakings I shall lie on this mattress sick; then, dead. . . . Where shall I be then?' I lifted my head and beheld the spotless orange light of the morning beaming up from the dark hills into the wide Universe."
—Ralph Waldo Emerson, October 21, 1837

A young man in a clean smock
hurries down a green corridor.
He clenches under one arm
an aluminum litter
on which a thin white old man
is strapped with heavy bandages.
The old man grimaces and squirms
and talks wildly about dying
and the problem of *here.*
He wants to know where here
will be when he is not here
and where the dear earth
with all its familiar things.
"I am what they are," he cries
"They are what I am, my home
the comfortable forms of myself.
How will they even exist
when I am not here?
Where will be the tissues
of sunset drifting among the trees?
and the mists gathering at the river
and that orange spinnaker moon
standing beyond the headland?
and where will be the galaxies
rising like tears in my eyes?

and where my ancient foes
scuffling in shadowy ceremony
kicking my skull
along the moonlit sand?
where the city where I used to live
close to the dark curve of earth
like a fingerprint of light?
and where my only lover
stretching
under the sheets of dawn
with the immortal smell of animal?"
But this thin white old man
talks wildly about the idea of death
not death itself. He is not dead.
He does not know any more
where he will be
when he is not here
than the ordinary mean kid
carrying him down the corridor
and no less than any Pharaoh knew
whose withered and embalmed desire
was carried aloft by thousands.
But where will this dear earth be
when we are not here to keep it home?

Fifty-seventh Street Beach

I did not want to go alone:
it was the evening of my life.
And so I waited for my friends.
I walked up and down the beach.
The sand was cold, the wind, clear
as glass, the traffic, sweeping
like a scythe around the Outer
Drive. In the southern sky
the glow of steel mills
was etched like a faded rose
and nearby, a troupe of Scouts
sang ditties, roasted their weenies
their faces shimmering on the wind
like pink globes of fetuses
prepared for now
      but not for always.
The waves were dark and cold.
And gradually my friends appeared
by starlight, curled in hollows of sand
on iron benches, along the fishing pier.
They were the last vacationers
their bodies soft & wrinkled
like old sleeping bags.

Singularity

Even when I lie
revealed
       like a bone
    in an old field
of sunshine

the hissing singleness
of things attacks me.

Therefore is
always the bright
excessive problem
of myself.

What had I done?
What had I done?

I cannot remember
anything
       but her
on the ninth day of March
      on the soiled bed
shrieking

         and me
fighting the blank sinewy
body of loneliness
and guilt

>   falling back
from my white vicious face
in the bathroom
mirror

>   falling back
>   between grey walls
funneling
>   down to a small window
>   broken, and ajar

>   falling
>   down and out
>   my face like white bark
off birches
>   blown
>   thru rotted grass
>   at evening, by the church
in the fog behind our house—

the gravestones
with their human names
>   standing cold and desolate
>   without love
in their irrevocable
singleness.

I cannot remember anything

but falling back
into my white face
in the mirror, falling back
thru that deep and singular world
seeking who I am.
Are we doomed to one and two
and three? Beyond the graves
the star begins to flare
warm and golden.
Will it be melting everywhere?

The Revolutionist, With Some Reference to the Student Revolution of 1970

"O had his powerful Destiny ordained
Me some inferiour Angel, I had stood
Then happie; no unbounded hope had rais'd
Ambition."

—*Paradise Lost* (IV: 59–61)

I

So now
it has begun
outside this time
among the others
who got done-in
sacked before
they were ever
born
         for whom
there are
no gifts
but those
they give
themselves
the violence
of translation
I have suffered
since childhood
that old defiance
thriving wanting out
in-rolling radiance
glinting out

the charred
clanging
the guying nerve
vibrating rage
incarnating
for the kill

II

(I bring back
the frank days
of warm July
the blue palm of sky
shadowy winds
running
on my arms
the round hills
of daisies
and the mists
in clouds
and colored chains
all that slow
and loving spell
of sun and moon
and moving shapes
of greenness
and the deep wood
of teasing fruit.)

III

A "natural man
desires happiness."
He surely pants for it
with depraved
fury
          bolts
his room
tears down
the rickety Z
          of escape
outside among
jagged structures
          under the sun
     willing for what
is vast to happen
more than war.

On warm
summer nights
I spot him
lurking
in the thin
dusty foliage
of vacant lots
or by sheeted lightning
on flat roofs
running
or deep in his own
backyard
behind a heap
of stones, thrashing.

He does not know
the matter.
He locked himself
outside, and dark
leathery fury
works him
like a razor.

IV

And so tonight
the others who
I nearly was
am, and nearly
            always will be
those new elect
with red helmets
and matted hair
stiffen
with the old
defiance
the thriving
            wanting out
and move out
(but not alone
like you and me)
but now in gangs
in corporation
across the park
to the hard rock
of perverse ritual.

And in shadows
under dead elms
in dead grass
the strays
are loving
small face here
small face there
fierce agitations
of colored space.

The Pirate: Secular Epiphany No. 2

I

I pole my blue boat
out of the hiding place
thru the drab fog of dawn
and with my shining cutlass
whack down the brown cattails
and coast out
by the sucking intake
and the piled rocks
whited by the gulls
I curse—
              and sail
along the northern shore
past the tattered brilliance
of the autumn trees
past drawn-up docks
and the locked cottages
standing in a strange light
of crying, then tack hard by
the little lighthouse
and hike out
into the great open lake
wrinkled and gray
under a gray
and wrinkled sky.

I am that pirate captain
swarthy and miraculous
with a terrible will
and no fear; and

this is my galleon blue
with its stout old hull
that I have sailed alone
all my crafty career
with stubbornness
and skill.

                   And I say
to myself, 'So what
tough guy?' and steady
the long glass to my eye
but sight no golden prize
no radiant horizon—
only flotsam of desire
dots the gray film of sea
and sky.
                   I have only
the discipline of the day
and the tiny song of me
to me.

II

But the weather changes
and I am lucky and I am new
and dauntless
and the little lighthouse
like my lady, stands
astute in colors
dashing
and spraying
along the tattered shore

and I am knotted in a hard body
that thrives on hard sailing
into hard wind.

I sneer, cry
and flail the whitecaps
with my shining cutlass, whack!
And on the last beat, far out
with the shore thrown away
I harden up fast and flat
with joy and pain

and from the fresh open lake
and soft wilderness
of waves

              we are lifted away
      my lady and I
in gusts of sun and rain—
burning flesh of sail whitening the bone

I and My Dark Friend

This warm wet
April annoys me
the heaved stones
the mildewed fences
the pruned bushes
dripping
like testicles
raked bibs
of suburban lawns.

I walk downtown
up white sidewalks
crisscrossing
by stoplights
blinking
orange, green
red, like flowers
in blocks of sunlight
full of white people.

Jonathan
you say "We
have no reason
            to doubt
that some of them
will burn in hell
to all eternity"
So where
do I go from here
            to lose myself
every day of my life?

Shall I go back
to a day too rainy
when I and my dark friend
killed rats
                creeping down
the black asbestos pipes
in our father's
basement
                shrieking
by guillotine
air-gun
and hammer?
                or back
to a freezing afternoon
at Stag Field
                when we
in the atomic cement stands
trapped alley cats
sparkling
and leaping from wall
to wall
        snatched at
them with stiff
hands?
        I squat
and slowly redden
with a last scream.

I cannot reach him now
but rise and shadow him
thru alleys, out of town
down long gravel roads
turn past the thin
color of dumps

smoldering
and nighthawks
in the late evening
and ground fog
                drifting
further than the gray
unpainted agony
of shanties
and the mules
and broken fences
black
      in the seething rain
and lie down with him
in tall spear grass
drifting
      among boulders
dark as men rising
and look back
at lights
of the tiny town.

A Deeper Image

When I jogged by Adler Planetarium
with its miniature machinery of stars
the western sky was a smudge of red lips
and moored yachts in Burnham Harbor
rocked in the reflected toothed
brilliance of the Chicago skyline.

But then I saw a deeper image
drifting under the surface like a grey
discarded sail or an old newspaper
with a photo of an abstract crime.
It was the vast undulating face
of starving African children.

My Dear Hobbes

"Life is but a motion of limbs."

—*Leviathan*, Part 1

I

I twisted
in the hair shirt
of heat
            and lay
and looked out at the stars
at the lighthouse
floating
on the gray cliff
above the dark river—
its revolving bright beam
fluttering
with shad flies, like angels
over the river of time—

over which came
cries of my late reading:
Foxe's great *Book of Martyrs*—
faint outmoded martyrdom
the strange eagerness
of Ridley and Latymer
scooping soft flame
to themselves
charring
the earth off
for the love of Christ—

II

Then I read in the great book *Leviathan*
about how the world and the beings in it
are big and little machines, how the life
of man is "solitary, poor, brutish, and short."
And here now my own lover comes to me
not like Christ in the withering light
of the stars, but naked and alone; and we
move together thru a dark world remoter
than a negative, driven by the yearning
for material things, by the beast trashing
the icons of eternity. We move our limbs
like hounds creeping by light of the moon
down the old cow path of despondency
thru scraggly wild black roses, past
the lighthouse with its yellow beam
following the inexplicable scent of birth
unto death, down to the churning river
where in the developing day, we squat
in heat on the granite shore, grunting
like pink new-born animals defecating
"the whole mass of [all] things that are."

The Lost Anchor: Secular Epiphany No. 3

I wade
at sundown
in springtime
among the long reeds
in the marsh water
cold to my thigh
to an old pier
near a green
boathouse
where I lost
the anchor
for my
blue scow.

I feel the black
suck of nothingness
and press my face
into my hands
and go over
those stories
of sweet otherness
I wanted open to—
over those harsh
justifications
that cannot work.

We learn to watch
each other die—
how we lose
hunger.

I am shrunk
to a ailing skin
among the long reeds
near a green boathouse
by an old pier—
sweeping with my hands
thru the black muck
for the anchor
I never use
any more—

       but
when I lift my face
into the eternal stillness
of the evening sky
the frogs
on their dark pads
among the long reeds
and blue vapors
of the moon
are calling to me
out of everywhere
and the marsh water
is warm and vibrant
to my thigh.

I Cannot Go

The heavy evenings
fester
with the lark.
            I cannot go
where we have gone before
not to the hollows of the hugging park
contagious shade
not to the gilded shore
fly-blown
with skeletons
of brown gymnastic lovers—
higgledy-piggledy
on the brittle waves
bounce
the amber rascals
of the sun.
            I cannot go
where we have gone before
not to the moonlit meadow
with all the clover motions
of your skin—
not to cyanic hills
where we have been
among the laurel in the great sunrise.

I crave you, but I cannot go
where we have gone before.

The Re-entry: Spring Time

And I was out
of place
         humped
to the dead wind
on the surface
of things
the flatness
and the absence
and the stars' acetylene
on that stark
and konked equipment
and how hard I ran
I could not move.

I drew
into myself
all winter
        pain
like keen spears.

And now I turn
and screwing
up my face
look out over
the thawed fields
of laughing stock
at the viking-blue
heaven:

           March!
and the winds blow.

I clap clap
my hands:
                    snow
            and anemic luster
the feathery glitter
gone!
      What fickle
thriving itch
is on me now
what lithe
& red gut
coiled
that I strut
cocksure?

            O blessed
is the sun swirling
like glycerin
that sports me
to the green
seething
underfoot whisperings
of evaporation
and embeds me
in warm rot
old leaves
color of armpits—
the tangle
and the urgency
I ever come back to.

The Path

I returned because I never left
that certain path leading down
to my father's boathouse
where I built my blue boat
to sail on forever on the river
rollicking in the sun. I returned
but wandered down a tangled path
to a small building by the water
with nothing in it but an old boat.
This happens in a lifetime.
On some invisible path
we move away from places
we believe we can never leave
places that invented with us
our own individual selves.
Now on this golden evening
I watch myself shuffling down
a path of shadows to the shore
now walking on the gilded waves
back and forth, back and forth.
In the offing, near the lighthouse
swirls the dark reef of good-bye.

Vita Update of a One-Time Pacifist

(In memory of my college roommate, Danny Goodman,
killed in the "Battle of the Bulge," 1944.)

Once drafted I refused to fight
for I was angry to be bothered
by a war, and prayed to God
they wouldn't clap me into jail.
But Danny whispered, "I will fight.
Such evil will invade, invade"
and waited for the final call—
but kept on keeping fun alive:
touch football with all the guys
and movies with his girl. At last
he shook my hand, saluted, left
forever—though in a dreamy way
I see him trotting back across
the moonlit campus to our dorm.
    The military mind inspected me
for signs, naked, and at length
with others of my fighting age
who wouldn't go, then ordered me
to do some work of public worth
to pick up sticks on nature's trails
and swab the johns in public parks—
then sent me to a state asylum
where I adjusted to my disbelief.
    I often strolled on summer nights
near those barracks of gray stone
barred, and strong enough to hide
the dirty pranks within, even
the monsters. When I wandered
beyond the institutional grounds

into the fields, to the little stream
filled with the brown slime of snails
the breeze from the barracks was laden
with the odor of human excrement
and in the green activity of the moon
the mosquitoes were as fierce
as machine-gun fire. I kept seeing
Danny's happy face being blow away.

    We all have our wars, but mine
was particularly tough, underhanded
and long-lasting. After my release
I researched Edwards for horror,
guilt, and revenge. Let any god
who made this world be crucified—
our very visions of heaven belie him.
Now I read Emerson to learn to cope
with solitude, to dream reality
to dream a world more real than this—
to love my foe, my monsters in the wing.

Note: This poem refers, in chronological order, to Danny Goodman, to
      my pacifist status in World War II, to my wartime government as-
      signments in the Great Smoky Mountain National Park, and then
      in Byberry State Mental Hospital near Philadelphia, and, finally, to
      my readings in and writings about the Calvinist minister, Jona-
      than Edwards, and Ralph Waldo Emerson, the American Tran-
      scendentalist.

Cat: Hit and Run

At seventy the cat was hit
as if a gased-up white-eyed god
banged the world while scooting home
eclipsing half the cat, then vanished
like a red-eyed fuming devil
down the concrete track. The cat
in spasms of amazement, licked
the crystal bubbles on its side
and dragged its back legs thru the snow
the front ones worked like skidding chains
to avoid Death. And the world
was shrieking as it waved its head
chaotically, and died.

The Thud

He cannot ever sleep
but tosses and untucks
himself, and starts up
scratches the frosty pane
and looks up at the stars
entangled in the trees

and hears again the thud
the softest thud of dog
on bumper, close to him
along the underneath
and settling far behind
humped like a beaded toy

and cannot understand
how any act so quick
and easy to himself
and out of his control
blanked the brisk world
for something else alive.

He hunches on the quilt
drowsy with deadly cold
and perished in himself
and all the lost outside
glitters with the heave
and withering of frost.

The Knot

(For R. G. Vliet, Barbara, Bill, Chris, Ed, Judy, Lew, Rod,
all dead or dying by cancer.)

I am sitting in the boathouse
among the boats I have hauled in
and carefully stowed away
the sunfish, the speedboat, and the dinghy.
I am sitting by the open door
on the gray boards
in the autumn sunlight
that strange light of crying
I have spoken to you about before.
I am trying to undo a knot in the bow
painter of my blue sailboat. I am
getting ready for the land of winter
for myth, for dark clouds, flurries
of snow translucent in the pale sun.
For I am also they who are dying
and I am putting away my boats
for a long time of loneliness
and grief among my friends, the time
before the time not easy to think about.

It Sticks in My Mind, Daddy

A cold April rain
when green is green
but not yet, and death
is a stone wall we seep
thru, like rain.
It sticks in my mind, Daddy
that sunny morning I was curled up
on the porch of our old home
by the river, watching
the rainbows of the dew
dripping off the gutter.
I was light-headed, softer
and cleaner than the summer
rain, and once more forgiven.
But then I heard a moo. I sprang
up, scrambled like crazy off the porch
over the granite, whirled down the path
(I was a skinny, coordinated little guy)
with my white T-shirt fluttering
flaying my arms, and yelling:
"The cows! the cows!
have gotten in past the gate, Daddy.
They're all plucking, chewing our grass
muddying the sweet waters of our bay.
Where's Tigger?" And then with me
hollering and slinging stones
and Tigger bouncing and yapping
at heifers and calves and the bull
all mooing and balling and snorting
we chased, Tigger and I, that whole herd
rocking and swaying out of our place
back thru the broken gate

back to where they belong, Daddy.
Don't you see now, crouching there
in the greenery behind the wall?
We did it again and again
for you.
                    What is the very real
when those we love, even the old
the mangled, and the dumb have gone
the way of rain, of silence?

Autumn Leaves

I walk over to the office
window near the gray files.
The autumn sunset blankets me
without warmth, and darkness
rises in the streets like debt.

In the distance flows on
the bloody river I came from.

Time to quit, to go back home.
Some rush the door, others
linger in pain.

When I was young
I could never get it right.
        but hung out savagely
in an old swamp of sunshine
nestling in bright density
piddling my time in the grass
waxing the exquisite lumber
of my blue boat.
                I moved
like stone. I was brown
ingrown & prickly.

But now tonight, I see
under the fluorescent lamp's curved neck
white hairs stiffen on my arms
and know
beneath my clothes
that my bare self displays
the wrinkled softness of old age.

I think of my casual friend
I had known all my life
who retired early
to his yellow cottage
on the swamp's far side
who sat by the river, like a frog
smoking, waiting for flies
and died in his sleep.

I stand by the window
and flex savagely. I calculate
the colored grid of traffic
flight, the dark country.

Where did it go
my beautiful blue boat
          of fugitive desire?
Where in the grassy darkness
do its black ribs lie?
Can it still build within me
with the bright blindness of youth?
Can it still breast my pale wrinkles
and weather the accurséd fear
of where the bloody river flows
the gray breeze of contrition?

I search the files
but do not find even a sign
or scrawled chart of its location.
I leave, and hurry off down the street.

I scout the fields
the woods, the moonlit river shore
the path wild creatures take to die alone
the dark swamp of my white face.

I do not know where else to go.
The river flows down to the sea.
My pockets are filled with charts
crumbling like autumn leaves.

When Roofs Will Not Be Needed Any More

I seek new leaks
in our summer home
by the river—but only
at night in stormy weather
sneaking in and out of rooms
with a weak flashlight, peering
for glisten on the bone-long rafters
for plops of rain in pottys and pans
and other signs of deluge seeping in—
the cold sogginess of soaked
blankets and wrinkled softness
in the cluttered notebooks
of love in my study
                  But only
in southwest wind and sunshine
do I work erotic on the leaking roof
scrambling almost naked
in ragged blue jeans
up to the cupola and gray flagpole
(with our flag of heaven & earth flying)
gazing down at the river's glittering wash
at my blue boat shivering on its chain
then kneeling on the ridge, drifting
in heat, in sheen
to the shriek of gulls
and barnstorming swallows
swatting wasps, slapping tar on
like honey, nailing down
green patches, dark scabs
             blown by the wind
over this incessantly decaying roof.

But in the evening, on the porch
rocking in my chair, I think
of death and oblivion
and sense a sweet
foreboding shift of wind—
my body glistens
and I lean forward, searching
          the distant skies
for the faint auroral lightning
                of that final storm
when roofs will not be needed any more.

Redemption

I

I woke
to the wrong
colorless daytime
of what cannot be true
and by the dull
power of loss
was driven
around and around
a lake of a silent black mistake
driven
to the soft drums
of what could have been.

The sameness was staggering.

Do the dead
know nothing of us
though they come
from here?

II

I sat
on a stone
in the cold rain
            and noticed
how the world
had no part of me.

I saw the end of time—

the brown spots of old age
        like lichen on my hands
the lumps of low cloud
        hurrying
                    the flocks
of screaming birds
                        rising
from the pale horizon
                of the neutral lake.

I saw the x-rays of the lightning
        flashing thru the hills

the wiry outlines
        burning and shrieking
on the far edge.

        I saw the stars
ascending with the cry and fur
        of violence.

and heard the booming of the earth.

III

I saw a figure
sitting
in the cold rain
beside me
     on a stone

a figure
I had surely known

a figure
who becomes me
all along
who shields me
from the vast Alone.

The True Sun: Secular Epiphany No. 4

"We are led to Believe a Lie
When we see not Thro' the Eye."

—William Blake

I

Earth is
what I can
              jump on
         out of myself
but only after
I am bound
in myself
and run
here and there
thru the tough night
exhibiting
the waxy anguish
of my brawn
to others
who recline
and pick apart
themselves
in flickers
by the water

     and only
after I figure
what on earth
they are about
their clean

feeling eyes
on me
        and me
all lean
for living

        and after
I come aware
that any way I go
the sharp trembling
situation of
my self
can only be
clenched in flesh
that even brilliant flesh
rots in the dark
and empty dawn
upon us all

        and only
after I know
I cannot guess
my home

        and know
that I am so alone
that I am far
beyond analysis
and any feeling
am never never
broken down

and know
that in such solitude
salvation is
at last.

II

And now
in this wild
        ramshackling
springtime
I lean back
        on an old zig-
zagging apple
fence
        and look out
at dainty fields
of daylight
drawn
with ease
on the crystal air
floating moisture with
tiny flowers pink
and exquisite
rootiness of frog
and gray lichen
soft swerve
of creature
behind
my bright eyes
        look further, far
beyond my self
where I draw

78

swinging
upon my breath
those cattails in
the thin blue silver
of that pond
                    dashed
to the yeeb-yeeb
of wild
ducks.
            And I rasp
      with a stone
stiff skin
      and rub in
            the grass
and shining dirt
and with a cry
hustle
with slow bounds
over the green edge.

The true sun
draws me
like a throb
and I am
caught alive
by ferocious green
and risen in the growth.

Reflections on Aging & Death

"That which does not
decay is so central in
us that as long as one
is alone by himself
he is not sensible
to the inroads of time
which always begin
at the surface—edges."

—Ralph Waldo Emerson

I

I am not that frayed
shape of skin and bones
deep in other eyes
but at the center
fresh as a daisy
and blue skies.

What I have done
I have done well.

And I resent
these wan hallucinations
of serenity; every firm
and lovely girl
abashes me with "Sir."

And I resent
these slow-motion shadows
climbing
        winter walls

this leathery limb
flailing
at yellow tennis balls
these vague
and quiet yawnings
for the summer bird
all these inane
gestures
            of gripping
into richness once again
this dying pastel
of what I used
to be.

Where is
what I once was?

How can
what is out there
be new again?

II

In the evening
I lean back
on the railing
of an old iron fence
and watch the red leaves
before an offshore
wind, flying out
        over the silver water

and glimpse
behind the dry ferns
in pools along the shore
my own reflections
of skin and bone.

In what season
will I die—
                    buried
        in flurries
or mucks of April?

III

I am one
among many
quiet persons
who await death
in this cell.

I am wrapped
in buffalo robes.

I doze off and on
and peer through bars
at the televised plain
of pure American
boredom.

I hear turkeys
and the cold bluff
of hell.
            I wave my arms

        for something real
to happen
            and the dull
yonder bursts alive
with fearful themes.

And there I go,
a broken-field runner
from god-knows-where
stretching beyond myself
across the windy heartland
thru shadows of clouds
in back of hummocks
zig-zagging
                to avoid
the radiant jackals
of disease.

I cross my fingers
but the carcass
crawls—
            the whole
outlandish veneer
is warping:
                plains
the blue mountains
the gorgeous palaces
in brain-like
tangles
            and even
my own lyttleness
like a bristling tree
is fading, fading
from the Eye.

I wave my arms with
out killing anything.

We will never be again
the persons who we are.

IV

I trudge at sunset
down an asphalt road.
in my foul-weather gear
swinging a kerosene lantern—
trudge by burnt wreckage
to the turn-off, trudge
along the dark crepe
of shore, and squat
among jewel weed
and soft stumps
of willow—
        and I search
      with my binoculars
    the wide glimmering waters
I have sailed and will sail on
in my blue boat
searching for the local place
and moment I will die.

But no logic, acid, Word
or hypothesis I know
can tell me
who I am
why I was born
when and where I was.

Beyond chance
and coherence, my face
emerges from the face
of God, my body born
from the radiance
of each day.

V

Is human knowledge
of death like flying
for pterodactyls
the dawn
of adaptation
to a new world
deep in the mirror
of my abstract eyes?

VI

I grip
the railing.
            Will it come
        now, now in the dark
luminescence of evening?

It will come in time.

That will be nothing
but fragments of bone
and ash in crevices
of rock, white scum
upon the water.

But will it come at all
        to the clear center
    of the frayed circle?